The Windows of
J.R.A

Poems about growing up with Juvenile Rheumatoid Arthritis

Jennifer Sullivan

BookLeaf
Publishing

The Windows of J.R.A © 2022 Jennifer Sullivan

All rights reserved.

Presentation by *BookLeaf Publishing*

Web: www.bookleafpub.com

E-mail: info@bookleafpub.com

ISBN: 9789357691789

First edition 2022

DEDICATION

I dedicate this book to my family and friends who have been there to support and uplift me through my worst battles.

Why my child?

I look through the window, to see storm clouds
looming.
A young girl crying through pain, in the darkest
of nights.
"It hurts", she says, "I can't move."

A mother and father looking for answers; that
remain questions.
"Why my child?"
"Is this a part of our history, part of the plan, part
of her future?"

She is a child,
suffering from an "Elderly Person's" disease.
Bones soft and bridle, easily broken.

Bending, not bending.
Painful, red and swollen.
Tears mixed with questions.

She is only 5 years old.
Rain, rain, go away.
Please protect this child today.

There's no Place like Home

Beep, Beep...shhhh...it's late.
Or maybe it's early.
Hospital sheets in a tangle.
Encasing me in this time capsule of pain.

"We're here to take your blood."
"Shhhh...don't cry, go back to sleep."

Dreams of red rivers,
Dreams of tin men
I need oil, I'm stuck.
Click, Click, Click, of my red ruby slippers.

"There's no place like home. There's no place
like home."

I open my eyes to see the nurses and hear the
cries.
I'm still a prisoner in this hospital gown.

Hospital windows.
I see outside, where other children are going to
school.
Children in school, writing me letters.
Saying they miss me.

Somewhere...somewhere over the rainbow;
There is a place where no child is sick.

Underwater

Physical therapy, Chiropractor, Acupuncture,
Exercise.

Keep your shoulders back,
Take your medicine.

My body is full of Gold,
I wish I felt rich.

Hot wax takes the shape of my bent fingers.
Gnarled like the bent limbs of a tree.

I hear the taunting laugh of the witch and her
spells,
Cursing me to a life filled with pain and
deformities.

Needles stick me like a pin cushion.
I'm their voodoo doll.

Water therapy with people four times my age,
talking about their Grandchildren and broken
hips.

Treading water, floating, sinking, sinking.
It's so peaceful under the surface, looking up
through the water.

A window of blurred reality.
I wish I could stay in this underwater world, my
body soft and weightless.

I start to rise to the top.
I need air.
Back to the weight of the world.

My Heroes

"You can do anything you want to do, you just
need to do it differently than everyone else."

They raised me to have confidence,
To be positive,
To try everything.
They loved me and worried about me.
And hid tears when they saw me struggle.

Days filled with encouragement and smiles,
nights filled with tears and prayers.

My father, always protecting me-
Lifting me above the waves,
Holding my hand,
digging his feet deep in the sand.

My mother beaming with pride-
watching me dance, play piano, ride my bike-
like all the other little girls.
A shadow of love and sadness on her face,
as I catch her staring out of the window at me.

I thank my parents for their loving
encouragement.
They fought so that I could be strong.

Rules

Skinny, shy, socially awkward.
I had friends, but never felt like I fit in.
Always on the outside of the circle.

I know they all had questions.
I know I was terrible at tennis,
And everything else athletic.

I was pretty much a regular teenager.
School, work, New Kids on the Block, singing
in the choir.
Buying the latest styles of Jordache jeans.

But, I could never play any sports.
I wanted to play soccer,
But, my Doctor said "No."
Skiing?...Definitely Not!

I was always a pretty good kid.
A rule follower.
Afraid to push boundaries,
Because I just may break.

Working at CVS

Friday: Four hour shift
Saturday: Eight hour shift
Sunday: Six hour shift
Monday: Can't get out of bed.

Bowling

Strike!

Bowling pins falling down like a group of
drunken schoolboys.
I'm laughing because of this victory.
Success after my bowling ball slowly rattled
down the lane
with my double-handed push.

That's the night he decided he loved me.
Over a game that needed an adjustment to the
rules.
He loves me because of my adjustments. My
ability to overcome!
I love him because he makes me laugh.

He tells me that I should not get the handicap
pass, walk it instead.
Live your life!
Don't give in.
He tells me I am strong!

We are married.
We are salt and pepper, a team.

Bowling ball and pins, rolling through this journey.
Falling down and getting back up again.

Mom

Dear Lord, protect my children,
keep them healthy and safe.
My evening prayer for the last 23 years.

Lord, make me walk with a cane,
make my life miserable with pain.
But protect my children from this suffering.

Thank you, Lord, for your blessings and answers
to my prayers.
A softball player.
A swimmer.

I love watching them grow.
They are healthy and strong
and a little bit mischievous.

I have never felt more powerful.
Giving birth, pushing life; fitful and crying into
this world.
Two beautiful children, created out of love.

Pieces of me, pieces of him;
swirled together into a beautiful Masterpiece.

Genetics be damned, stay away from my family tree.

Every Spring, Summer, Winter and Fall,
The seasons of Motherhood,
have been the best of them all.

Years of guiding my children, teaching them,
burying myself in their presence.
My precious children, full of energy and life, I
stay healthy for them.
"Mom" is my favorite word in the world.

Barbie

Modern Science, taking out my disease and
replacing it with plastic.
Where cartilage has vanished, they create a new
joint.
Part human, part doll.
My anti-theft tag beeps through security.
Announcing to everyone that I have an intrusion
of parts.
Feeling lucky that I am walking through the
airport,
Pushing a case, instead of a chair.

Count backwards from ten and wake up with a
new hip.
Stitches torn, exercise.
A rebirth.
Learning again how to walk, how to sit.
Skills that most of us take for granted.
I was the nurse's favorite patient.
I was young and hopeful.
"Can we play with your hair? Let's talk".
A thirty-year-old mother in Orthopedics.
"You'll be back," they say, "in about 30 years."
The life expectancy of a plastic hip.

Battles

Battles between Patriots and the British,
The Left and the Right.
White blood cells constantly attack the enemy.
But who is the enemy?
The cells do not know.

Lessons

Do you understand the context?
Can you multiply and divide?
Lessons in school,
students competing for the answer.

I teach them how to read and write.
But I also teach lessons about life.
Have compassion.
Help those in need.
Be kind.
Their teacher needs all of these things.
Don't judge others.
Ask questions.
The most important lessons, tested outside of the
room.

I share my story and they understand.
Inspire.
Empower.
Little voices that will change the World.

The Weather Forecast

Cloudless, sunny days.
Nights with never-ending rain.
My joints predict the weather.

My ankle whispers, "Bring the umbrella."
My fingers shout, "Pack the gloves."

Maybe someday I'll move to Arizona.
Where the days are hot and dry.
Is that the special place where my joints won't complain?

Ankle braces and air foam sneakers.
Beds too soft, beds too hard.
All of these elements are as crazy as the forecast.

When will I find my "just right"?

He Spoke

Judgement.
Prejudice.
Closed-minded.
No sense of humor.
My first experience in the career world.
"You have a weak handshake", he said.
"But I have a strong voice", I thought.
"Will Arthritis affect your performance in this
career?", he asked.
"Not unless I have to play on the company
softball team," I joked.
"You're fired."

He Spoke.

Growing Old

He complains about growing old.
"Oh, my back hurts, my muscles ache.
I can't play golf like I used to."

The people I love are catching up to me.
The ones who have cared for me and helped me,
Are facing their new reality.

Aging is hard.
It's all I've ever known.

A young spirit trapped in an ancient tomb.
What will the future hold when the strong
become weak?
Will I be met with resentment? Or a deeper
understanding?

Aging is hard.
I know what you will need to overcome.

I've lived in this way for as long as my memory
stretches.
I pray that we can grow old gracefully.
As companions. As friends.

Wishes

I wish I could wear high heels.
I wish I could take ballet.
I wish I could hike up the mountain.
And ski back down, all the way.

I wish I could fly an airplane,
like in the movie "Top Gun".
I wish I could perform on Broadway.
A dancer like Gwen Verdon.

I wish I could relax with yoga.
Bend my body like a trapeze,
I wish I could ride a pony.
I wish I could love him with ease.

I could let these wishes consume me,
Give in with a sigh of defeat.
Instead I reflect and remember
True moments that make me complete.

The Skeleton

Two bones rubbing each other the wrong way.
The pillow of cartilage long disappeared.

Ghostlike outlines flickering on the screen.
Reminding me that pain is invisible.

The doctor can see the destruction,
But cannot feel the hurt.

The body is so much more than the skeleton.

Addicted to pain

The camera shutter keeps clicking, every time I
blink.
Taking snapshots of this constant desire.

My body signaling that the time is drawing near.
Relief is on the horizon,
one more hour of uncomfortable poses.
Ungraceful images.
A tired model, waiting for the end of her shoot.

The capsule slides down my throat,
I can feel the roots of relief,
reaching out to heal me.
Images become fuzzy,
like the world is now out of focus.
Easing my pain, Click!

Strength

How does one define Strength?
Where does it come from?
Is it Fear
Vanity
Hope

Like the moon pulling in the tide,
my strength is internal, a force invisible to the
human eye.
But felt, like waters rushing to the shore.

My strength is survival.
For how long will I handle this weight?
When will I start to deflate?
A balloon soaring high, will eventually decline,
releasing air upon its return.

I become weaker with every step.
Life quickly passing me by.
Slow down I shout,
I cannot keep up.

Trying to make it through another day.
How long before my body surrenders
And I no longer have the strength to walk.

Windows

Walking along the cobblestones,
I look up towards the light.

A variety of windows.
Some curtained in privacy,
others calling out to come join the fun.

I see a man hunched over a canvas,
pouring out his soul with a paintbrush of color.
I see women laughing over a spilled bottle of
wine.
There is a shadow behind that curtain,
a twirling figure, excited to see what the night
has in store.
There is a couple dancing, they know each other
so well
that their feet just move to the beat.
In that window, a woman is crying
after hearing life-altering news.

We all have our windows in this life.
Challenges that we want to hide behind
and celebrations we share with the world.
Let's not just pass by and window shop.
Let's open them up and let in fresh air.
Because a life without windows will be Stifling.